P9-EMG-218

DAVID BECKHAM

SPORTS STARS
who give back

GIFTED AND GIVING SOCCER STAR

by J Chris Roselius

E **Enslow Publishers, Inc.**
40 Industrial Road
Box 398
Berkeley Heights, NJ 07922
USA
http://www.enslow.com

Library of Congress Cataloging-in-Publication Data
Roselius, J Chris.
  David Beckham : gifted and giving soccer star / J Chris Roselius.
      p. cm. — (Sports stars who give back)
  Includes bibliographical references and index.
  Summary: "A biography of British soccer player David Beckham, focusing
on his philanthropic activities off the field"—Provided by publisher.
  ISBN 978-0-7660-3587-4
  1. Beckham, David, 1975—Juvenile literature. 2. Soccer
players—England—Biography—Juvenile literature. 3.
Philanthropists—England—Biography—Juvenile literature. I. Title.
        GV942.7.B432R67 2010
  796.334092—dc22
  [B]
                                    2009026186

Printed in the United States of America

102009 Lake Book Manufacturing, Inc., Melrose Park, IL

10 9 8 7 6 5 4 3 2 1

To Our Readers: We have done our best to make sure all Internet addresses in this book were active and appropriate when we went to press. However, the author and the publisher have no control over and assume no liability for the material available on those Internet sites or on other Web sites they may link to. Any comments or suggestions can be sent by e-mail to comments@enslow.com or to the address on the back cover.

♻ Enslow Publishers, Inc. is committed to printing our books on recycled paper. The paper in every book contains between 10% to 30% post-consumer waste (PCW). The cover board on the outside of each book contains 100% PCW. Our goal is to do our part to help young people and the environment too!

Photo credits: Haraz N. Ghanbari/AP Images, 1; Tammie Arroyo/AP Images, 8; Jennifer Graylock/AP Images, 11, 94; Fred Duval/FilmMagic/Getty Images, 16; Aris Messinis/AP Images, 21; AP Images, 25, 46, 90; Roberto Pfeil/AP Images, 31; Mark J. Terrill/AP Images, 37; Giuseppe Calzuola/AP Images, 39; Sean Dempsey/AP Images, 44; Rui Viera/AP Images, 53; Adam Butler/AP Images, 56; Ricardo Mazalan/AP Images, 64; Ruben Mondelo/AP Images, 70; Domenico Stinellis/AP Images, 72; Fernando Bustamante/AP Images, 76; John Giles/AP Images, 80; Jason DeCrow/AP Images, 84; Owen Humphreys/AP Images, 99; Antonio Calanni/AP Images, 109

Cover Photo: Haraz N. Ghanbari/AP Images

CONTENTS

COMING TO AMERICA

Stunning news made headlines around the world in January of 2007. David Beckham was coming to America to play soccer.

The English soccer star was also a global celebrity, known as much for his dazzling free kicks as for his often-changing hairstyles. His past two teams, Manchester United in England and Real Madrid in Spain, were among the biggest and most famous sports teams in the world. The midfielder had played in three World Cups and was a former captain of England's national team. Off the field, he was married to one of the singers in the popular '90s music group the Spice Girls, and the couple was constantly in the news.

BECKHAM BIO

Full Name: David Robert Joseph Beckham
Place and Date of Birth: Leytonstone, England, May 2, 1975
Parents: Sandra and Ted
Sisters: Joanne and Lynne
Wife: Victoria
Children: Brooklyn, Romeo, and Cruz

Now he was coming to play with the Los Angeles Galaxy, a team in Major League Soccer (MLS). This league was barely a decade old and had practically no following outside of the United States. It had also struggled at times to get attention within the country. Now, suddenly one of the most famous athletes in the world would be playing in MLS. "David Beckham coming to the United States is . . . [like] Tiger Woods meeting Brad Pitt on the red carpet," wrote *USA Today* sports columnist Christine Brennan. "This transcends sports. This is a big, big deal."[1]

Critics of the move said Beckham was heading to Los Angeles for the money. After all, his contract was a reported five-year deal worth as much as $250 million, with endorsements. Beckham would also receive a share of the Galaxy's jersey sales and ticket revenue. But Beckham had already made enough money to last several lifetimes during his career with Manchester United and Real Madrid. Money was not the reason he was coming to the United States.

According to Beckham, he decided to come to the United States because he wanted to make a lasting impact, to make a difference on the game in this country. Although soccer is gaining in popularity in the United States, its following still does not come close to that of football, baseball, or basketball. But on the youth level, soccer is one of the most popular sports in the country. Beckham believed in the sport's huge potential. He knew he could help turn soccer into a mainstream U.S. sport.

"I'm not saying me coming to the States is going to make soccer the biggest sport in America," Beckham said. "But . . . if I didn't believe that I could make a difference and take soccer to a different level, then I wouldn't be doing this."[2]

Beckham said he wanted to play in the United States for the kids. "There are so many great sports in America," he said. "There are so many kids that play baseball, American football, basketball. But soccer is huge all around the world apart from America, so that's where I want to make a difference with the kids."[3]

DID YOU KNOW?

Beckham wears a new pair of $500 soccer shoes for every game he plays.

LOOKING TO BOOST RATINGS

While Beckham was hoping to increase the overall popularity of soccer, MLS Commissioner Don Garber was more concerned with the player's effect on the league. Garber hoped Beckham would be a huge boost to not only the Galaxy but to every team in the league. "David Beckham is a global sports icon who will transcend the sport of soccer in America," Garber said. "His decision to continue his storied career in Major League Soccer is testament to the fact that America is rapidly becoming a true 'Soccer Nation' with Major League Soccer at the core."[4]

Garber was right. For weeks after the announcement, sports talk shows chattered about Beckham and MLS. Ticket sales in Los Angeles increased immediately, and teams playing host to the Galaxy were seeing their games sell out. "We sold 5,000 season tickets in less than forty-eight hours," said Tim Leiweke, president of the Anschutz

DID YOU KNOW?

Beckham came close to signing with AC Milan of Italy instead of the Galaxy in 2007. He has said he has always been a fan of Milan, and he would eventually join the Italian team on loan in 2009.

Entertainment Group, which owns the Galaxy. "And I'm like, I can't believe what just happened here."[5]

Before Beckham's arrival, some people had complained that MLS lacked star power. Many believed that, without a lot of well-known players, the league was subpar and so not worth watching. But Alexei Lalas, the Galaxy's general manager at the time, felt the arrival of Beckham and the following media spotlight would show just how good the quality of play in the league was. "One of the interesting things that I think people are going to see, is first off, the attention he's going to bring to the sport and to American soccer," Lalas said. "People are going to see the quality that exists over here."[6]

THE "BECKHAM RULE"

Unlike most soccer leagues around the world, MLS has a salary cap for each team. The league maintains the cap by owning all of the players' contracts. In other leagues around the world, the team owns the players' contracts. In November 2006, the salary cap for each MLS team was approximately $2 million. In the world of professional sports, that was not very much. Some individual players in Europe were making more money per season than an entire roster of MLS players made. With such a tight cap, it would have been impossible to ever sign Beckham

Beckham displays his new Galaxy jersey.

or any other European or Central American star who was still in the prime of his career.

To grow, the league needed to sign players the casual American soccer fan had heard of, such as Beckham. So the league's Board of Governors decided to relax the salary cap restriction by allowing each team to sign one player for any amount of money, with only the first $400,000 counting against the salary cap.

MLS called this the "Designated Player Rule." But to many in the press and to fans around the country, it is known as the "Beckham Rule." The Galaxy was the first team to take advantage of the Designated Player Rule and immediately created an international event when it signed Beckham.

> **"David Beckham will have a greater impact on soccer in America than any athlete has ever had on a sport globally."**
>
> *—Tim Leiweke*

Cheering fans could not get enough of Beckham during his first press conference in Los Angeles. It seemed he was on the cover of every magazine and the lead story in newspapers' sports sections around the country. "David Beckham will have a greater impact on soccer in America than any

A record 66,237 fans watched Beckham and the Galaxy play the Red Bulls in New York.

athlete has ever had on a sport globally," Leiweke said. "David is truly the one individual that can build the bridge between soccer in America and the rest of the world."[7]

YEARS IN THE MAKING

Many soccer fans were shocked when they learned of Beckham's deal with the Galaxy. But the news should not have really come as a surprise. For several years Beckham had been talking publicly about finishing his career in the United States. Leiweke had started to pave the eventual move to the United States as far back as 2003 when he helped Beckham start soccer academies in London and Los Angeles.

In 2005, Real Madrid played a "friendly," or exhibition game, against the Galaxy in front of a sold-out crowd. After the game, Beckham was asked about the possibility of ever playing in the United States. His answer should have provided a clue about his future. He told *Sports Illustrated*, "Playing in the

WANTING TO FIT IN

When joining the Los Angeles Galaxy, Beckham said he wanted to fit in with the team and get to know the players on a personal level, not just as teammates. He said he had felt he was part of a family with Manchester United, where he and several teammates had been playing together since their days on the youth team.

PLAYING WITH THE BEST

Beckham has played with a number of superstars. Of all these, he said the best was Zinedine Zidane of France. The two were teammates at Real Madrid.

MLS definitely interests me. If that can carry on with soccer games all over America, that's what I'd like to achieve."[8]

In May, England's national team went on to play in packed stadiums across the United States. Afterward, MLS Deputy Commissioner Ivan Gazidis also hinted about what a player like Beckham could do for the league and soccer in general. "We have 65 million people that are connected [by] soccer in this country, but they're not rabid yet," he said. "That's the challenge and the opportunity of soccer in the United States, and it's the challenge and the opportunity for David Beckham in the United States, the same way it is for Major League Soccer. Whoever is able to connect and activate the massive potential fan base wins. And if Beckham can do that, and if Beckham can help Major League Soccer do that, those are the kind of marriages made in heaven."[9]

The only bad news for the Galaxy was that the announcement came in January, but Beckham would not be able to play for the team until July. Beckham and Real Madrid still had several more months left in the Spanish La Liga season.

Beckham Mania was going to have to wait.

GROWING UP IN ENGLAND

David was born just outside London in the cozy suburb of Leytonstone. Nothing about his birth on May 2, 1975, would lead people to believe that David would someday be one of the most popular athletes in the world.

David was the second child of Ted and Sandra Beckham. The parents were thrilled to add a boy to the family, joining his older sister Lynne. For Ted, it was a chance to extend his love of soccer, which is called football in England. Ted was a huge fan of Manchester United, and he was ready to share his passion with his new son.

After a few years, the family moved to Chingford. As David grew up, Ted spent his free time taking David to the park to kick the ball around. David latched onto the sport in no time and would practice on his own for hours before playing with his dad.

At Chase Lane Primary School, Beckham was already showing his soccer skills. While also interested in art, it was soccer that David cared about the most. His ability improved as he grew older. Along the way Ted was there to encourage and help him in any way possible. Ted played for a local club and David was always at the games. A solid player himself, Ted made sure David always practiced his fundamental skills, like dribbling and passing the ball and taking free kicks. He did not want his son to be a one-dimensional player who could only shoot the ball.

"If you weren't playing well, [Dad] would tell you [that you] were rubbish and needed to do better," David said. "But he wasn't one of those dads who stood on the touchline [sideline] screaming. He had a softness about him as well."[1]

SHOWING OFF HIS TALENT

When he was seven, David joined a local youth club called the Ridgeway Rovers. His amazing talent was apparent from the very beginning. He scored more than 100 goals during his first three years with the club.

DID YOU KNOW?

When Beckham was only a toddler, his father made balls out of rolled-up socks for him to kick around the house.

Ted Beckham wanted his son to be more than a one-dimensional player.

But David was not just starring for the Rovers. He also played against adults in five-on-five games at nearby Wadham Lodge. On the field, David was just another soccer player, not a boy who was trying to compete against adults. And that is just the way Ted wanted it for his son. "[Dad] warned me that I had to be prepared to get a bit roughed up now and again," David said. "If he'd been running around telling people not to tackle me all evening, it would have been pointless me being there in the first place."[2]

David's talent was not a local secret. Despite being so young, London clubs Arsenal and Tottenham Hotspur were already keeping track of the young player. David was pleased that the two teams were showing interest in him. Even though he lived closer to Arsenal and Tottenham, David still cheered wildly for Manchester United. His friends often made fun of him for doing so.

In 1985, when he was ten, David competed at the Bobby Charlton Soccer Skill Tournament in Manchester, England. The tournament lasted a week and allowed David to compete against some of the best players in England, many of whom were older. David proved he could hold his own with the players and left a strong impression on Charlton, a legendary

ARSENAL FILE

Founded: **1886**
Location: **Holloway, North London**
Stadium: **Emirates Stadium**
Colors: **Red and white**
Nickname: **Gunners**

former soccer player who had once starred for Manchester United.

David was invited back to the tournament the next year and put on a show that many competitors remember today. Competing at Old Trafford, the same stadium where Manchester United plays, David won the skills competition and showed off his ability during games. "We were both eleven in our first proper football contest and David desperately wanted to start off with a goal," said Nana Boachie, who also attended the camp with David. "As a goalie on the opposing side, I wanted to keep a clean sheet. He just said 'We'll see,' in that quiet voice of his. Just before halftime, we gave away a free kick just outside the [penalty] area. David curled the ball into the top corner. It was impossible to save."[3]

By winning the skills competition, David earned a trip to Barcelona, Spain. He would spend two weeks training with FC Barcelona and Manager Terry Venables, a former standout player. Soon, soccer clubs from all over were interested in David. Tottenham Hotspur, located only minutes from his home, continued its pursuit of David and

⭐ THE MASCOT

"We used to bring him to games in London—he was our mascot at West Ham when he was twelve."

—*Manchester United manager Sir Alex Ferguson on David Beckham, who grew up near West Ham's stadium in East London* persuaded him to spend some time at their school of excellence.

But David spent most of his time training with Leyton Orient, a small club in the area. Soon, however, David would get the visit of a lifetime. During training, a scout from Manchester United approached him. "I can still remember the rush of joy and excitement," David said. "There was relief in there too. I burst into tears on the spot, just cried and cried. I couldn't believe how happy I felt. I'd wondered for such a long time if I'd ever hear those words."[4]

> "I burst into tears on the spot, just cried and cried. I couldn't believe how happy I felt."
>
> —David Beckham

A BIG DECISION

By 1991, when David was sixteen, he was seemingly drawing interest from every club in England. But David wavered between his two top choices,

TOTTENHAM HOTSPUR FILE

Founded: **1882**

Location: **Tottenham, North London**

Stadium: **White Hart Lane**

Colors: **White and navy**

Nickname: **Spurs**

Tottenham and Manchester United. Even though Manchester United was David's favorite team, Tottenham was only fifteen minutes away from David's home. He would be able to enjoy the support of his family and friends if he selected Tottenham, who are also called Spurs.

David felt it was only fair to visit with both clubs. He first visited with Tottenham at White Hart Lane, the team's stadium and headquarters. There he talked with John Moncur, the club's youth developing officer, and with Venables, who was now working for Tottenham. The London club offered David a

SAYING HELLO SEALS THE DEAL

At sixteen, when David visited Manchester United, manager Sir Alex Ferguson came over to Beckham and said hello. That simple gesture made a big impression on Beckham and he soon signed with the club.

Longtime Manchester United manager Sir Alex Ferguson talks to Beckham in 2002.

six-year contract, but he left the meeting with an uneasy feeling. He felt Venables did not remember him from his two-week training session in Barcelona.

David then visited Manchester United and got a much different reception. United manager Sir Alex Ferguson made David feel welcomed and wanted from the very beginning. When the meeting was over, United offered David a six-year contract as well. It did not take him long to decide he wanted to play for Manchester United.

David, sixteen, was now an official Manchester United trainee.

3

STARTING HIS CAREER

Beckham's childhood dream came true when he signed as a trainee with Manchester United in July of 1991. He was now a member of one of the world's most famous soccer clubs. David's father, however, made sure his son did not start to think he was better than everyone else. He made David continue to find summer jobs and often reminded the teenager that he was still just a boy who had not really started his career. "You may have signed for Man United, but you haven't done anything yet," said Ted Beckham. "When you've played for the first team, then we can talk about you having achieved something. Until then, don't start thinking you've made it."[1]

David might have been a trainee at Manchester United, but he was still a teenager. While home one summer, Ted made David get a job as a busboy at a restaurant and lounge near Chingford. It was a good thing David had enormous talent on the soccer field, because his work as a busboy did not leave a very positive impression on the owner. "His mind was never on the job he should've been doing, which was picking up the glasses," Val Yerral said. "I would say, 'C'mon, pick up some glasses!' Then I would say, 'What are you talking about?' And he'd say, 'Football.' He was always on about football."

SOCCER STRUCTURE

Since soccer is played in countries all around the world, there are many different leagues and tournaments. England is no exception, where the Football Association (FA) governs the various leagues and tournaments as well as the national teams.

The top league in England is the English Premier League (EPL), also known as the Premiership. But that's not the only league in England. The three last-place finishers in the EPL are relegated to a lower league, called the Championship, while the top three teams from the Championship are promoted to the Premiership. This promotion-relegation system connects dozens of teams throughout England, meaning even amateur and semi-professional teams could someday advance to the Premiership.

Additionally, there are two major tournaments in English club soccer—the FA Cup and the League

Cup—and many other smaller tournaments. The FA Cup is open to all teams in England, from amateur to EPL, and is considered the most important tournament in the country. More than 700 teams competed in the 2008-09 FA Cup. The League Cup (often known by the name of its sponsor, such as Carling Cup, Worthington Cup, or Coca-Cola Cup) includes the ninety-two teams that make up England's top four leagues.

Finally, there are international tournaments as well. In Europe, which is governed by UEFA, the top teams from each country play in the UEFA Champions League. The next best play in the Europa League, which used to be called the UEFA Cup. The winner of the UEFA Champions League then competes against the top teams from the other continents at the FIFA Club World Cup. FIFA is the world governing body of soccer.

MOVING UP

Beckham had to wait before playing with the senior club, or first team, but he quickly found success with the youth team. With the talents of future Manchester United stars Ryan Giggs, Gary Neville, Paul Neville, and Paul Scholes, United's youth team won the FA Youth Cup in 1992.

Only a few months later, Beckham was promoted to the senior club for a League Cup match against Brighton & Hove Albion. He was just seventeen.

Ryan Giggs controls the ball for Manchester United during a game in 2009.

Starting the game on the bench, Beckham soaked in the action and atmosphere. He barely believed he was playing for his favorite team. With only seventeen minutes left in the contest, Beckham made his Manchester United debut when he replaced Andrei Kanchelskis.

The euphoria Beckham experienced in that first game would have to last him for a while. It would be nearly two years before he would play with the senior team again. Until then, Beckham would remain with the reserve team, or second team, with his rapid rise to fame seemingly stuck in neutral.

He earned another shot with the first team in 1994. Beckham made his first full appearance against Port Vale in a League Cup match on September 21. He played in a few more League Cup games and then against Galatasaray of Turkey in a Champions League contest. Manchester United dominated the match, winning 4–0. One of those goals came on a blast by Beckham. It was his first goal with the Manchester United Red Devils.

ON HIS WAY OUT?

Despite the success he had against Galatasaray, Beckham was unable to stick with the senior team. He found

HE SHOOTS, HE SCORES!

Beckham had a memorable moment in his first Champions League game. Facing Galatasaray of Turkey, Beckham scored his first Manchester United goal. His first goal in the English Premier League came in the first game of the 1995–96 season against Aston Villa. It was the Red Devils' only goal of the game in a 3–1 loss.

himself playing for the reserve team before he was loaned to Preston North End, a small club that played in the third division. It was a world away from the big stadiums and bright lights of the Premiership.

Beckham was nervous about the loan, knowing such a move was often the first step to being sold to another team outright. "I knew [David] was worried [about being loaned to Preston]," said longtime teammate Gary Neville, who was receiving plenty of playing time with Manchester United at the time. "We all knew he had great ability but people said he was a bit soft going into tackles and headers."[2]

Beckham was thinking the worst. "They want to get rid of me," Beckham remembers thinking.[3] Ferguson assured the midfielder that he had a place at Manchester United. But before the young player could take that place, Ferguson wanted Beckham to get more playing time in meaningful games and not toil away on the reserve team, which played a lighter schedule.

Feeling better about the situation, Beckham headed to Preston North End. He entered his first

PLAYING WITH FUTURE STARS

When Beckham joined Manchester United, several of his teammates from the 1992 FA Youth Cup team became stars for the senior team. Beckham played with Ryan Giggs, Gary and Paul Neville, and Paul Scholes. These players were vital to Manchester United's success in the 1990s and into the new millennium.

game as a second-half substitute and scored against the Doncaster Rovers. Beckham scored 2 goals in his first five games. The second goal came against Fulham on a free kick, something he would master during his career.

"I think David thought he was on the way out," Ferguson said. "We had to convince his family because he was quite a young lad at the time, quite rakish. After a few weeks, he thought [playing with Preston] was fantastic."[4]

Beckham made a strong impression on his teammates at Preston North End. They admired his low-key demeanor. "He was driving a Ford Escort, was wearing an ordinary tracksuit and was a very shy lad who you wouldn't look twice at in the street," said former Preston North End teammate Simon Davey. "It was pretty obvious from the first training session with us that he was something special, but we had no idea just how special he would become."[5]

Said former teammate Ryan Kidd: "Back then Paul Raynor was in charge of free kicks and corners for Preston,

> **"It was pretty obvious from the first training session with us that he had something special, but we had no idea just how special he would become."**
>
> —Simon Davey

so he wasn't impressed when our manager Gary Peters pushed him to one side in favor of this kid we've never heard of. He told us Beckham was taking free kicks in training for United ahead of [established stars] Ryan Giggs and Denis Irwin. We thought he was pulling our leg."[6]

Beckham's goal against Fulham turned out to be his last for Preston North End. After only four weeks and five games, Ferguson decided Beckham had received the seasoning he needed and wanted him ready for Manchester United's match against Leeds United. When Beckham learned he was headed back to Manchester, he felt the news was bittersweet. "I've had some amazing experiences since but, truthfully, that month at Preston was one of the most exciting times in my whole career," Beckham said. "I remember thinking then that if the boss had been looking to let me go, I could have been happy playing with Preston North End. When it came time, at the end of the loan, to go back to United, I didn't want to leave. . . . Just four weeks later and here I was asking Mr. Ferguson if I could go and stay with them for another month."[7]

BACK WITH MANCHESTER UNITED

Ferguson believed Beckham was ready for the rigors of playing in the EPL. But he wanted to take the club in a different direction. After winning the EPL title in 1992–93 and the EPL and FA Cup in the 1993–94

YOUNG PLAYERS CAN'T WIN?

"You can't win anything with kids," TV broadcaster Alan Hansen exclaimed after Manchester United lost its first game of the 1994–95 season. Aided by Beckham's 8 goals that season, United won the English Premier League title and the FA Cup.

season, the Red Devils failed to win a single trophy in the 1994–95 campaign. Ferguson decided it was time to give his younger players a chance to shine. Several players were let go during that offseason. One of those players was Kanchelskis, creating a spot in the starting lineup for Beckham.

The 1995–96 season started with a loss against Aston Villa, despite a goal by Beckham. The defeat brought scorn from some in the press who said Manchester United could not win anything with a bunch of kids. Those kids, however, would prove their critics wrong. Manchester United was trailing Newcastle United by twelve points in the standings that January. They ended up winning the Premiership a few months later.

The Red Devils' streak was aided in part by Beckham, who scored 8 goals that season. In the second-to-last game of the season against Nottingham Forest, the Red Devils claimed a 5–0 win as Beckham scored 2 goals. Manchester United then won its

Beckham marks a player from German team Borussia Dortmund in a 1997 Champions League game.

season finale against Middlesbrough to claim the EPL title. "We just kept coming in for training, tuning up for games and were all on the kind of high which has you half expecting things to go wrong at any minute," Beckham said. "In the United first team? Winning the Premiership? There had to be a catch. But there wasn't. Instead, it got better and better."[8]

A RISING STAR

"You cannot afford to let things go to your head," David Beckham said. "First of all you'd get hammered by the other lads. Then you have to face up to the boss. The first sign that you're getting carried away and he comes down like a ton of bricks. I know how difficult it's been just breaking into the first team and I'm not going to do anything to put that at risk . . . I would be stupid to think I'm something special."[1]

Beckham might have told himself that he was not something special, but those who watched him play thought differently. Take, for example, the 1996–97 EPL season opener against Wimbledon.

A GOAL TO REMEMBER

On a cool August day, Manchester United controlled the game from start to finish, holding a 2–0 lead late in the game. Beckham gained control of the ball near midfield. Looking down the field, he noticed Wimbledon goalkeeper Neil Sullivan was far off the goal line, leaving the goal unattended. Beckham decided to drill a shot from the midfield line. Amazingly, the ball sailed over Sullivan's head and into the goal, stunning everyone in the stadium.

The goal was shown on highlight shows for weeks and was named the goal of the year after the season. "I've always been able to score goals, from Sunday League through youth level and the reserves, and now I'm getting my chance with the first team," Beckham said. "The Wimbledon goal is my favorite as it was different to all the rest and the one I enjoyed the most. That gave me a taste for long shots and now every one I hit seems to go in. My dad has told me to shoot on sight, from anywhere, it doesn't matter what happens. . . . I won't be scared to have a go."[2]

DID YOU KNOW?

Beckham made his first home appearance in the English Premier League against Leeds United.

JOINING THE NATIONAL TEAM

One month later, Beckham received some outstanding news. He was going to get the chance to represent England in a World Cup qualifier. Beckham was barely able to contain his excitement. Ferguson quickly offered advice to Beckham. "If you get the chance, play well. Just play like you have been doing for us at United," Ferguson said.[3]

In his national team debut, Beckham proved he belonged on the field as England took on Moldova. Beckham had had one strong practice session after another leading up to the match, and he now carried that performance into the game, helping set up 2 goals in a 3–0 win. The strong showing led manager Glenn Hoddle to select Beckham to play in every qualifying match leading up to the 1998 World Cup in France. Despite his outstanding play on the field, Beckham remained humble when it came to his success with the national team and with Manchester United.

"It has surprised me, from the first game of the season right up to now," Beckham said. "I've played most of United's games and three for England. I pinch myself every day as it's hard to believe how well everything has gone. You wake up and have things

DID YOU KNOW?

Beckham made his first appearance with the English national team on September 1, 1996 against Moldova.

around you that you never thought you'd have at twenty-one—your home, car, and all that. It's unbelievable."[4]

WORLD-WIDE ATTENTION— GOOD AND BAD

Fans and, more importantly, players from around the world started to take notice of Beckham and his rise toward superstardom. In the days leading up to a match against Italy at the famed Wembley Stadium in London, Italian goalkeeper Angelo Peruzzi said Beckham was a player to keep an eye on. Beckham found the praise flattering.

At the same time, Beckham was becoming more comfortable in the spotlight and surrounded by the media. Shy by nature, it was not easy for Beckham to get used to all of the attention that he was now receiving. "He is very level-headed and has a massive future if he maintains that [quality]," England manager Hoddle said. "If he stays along those lines he'll be a massive bonus for English football."[5]

Although Beckham was maturing as a player and a person, he still had one flaw that held him back at times. That flaw was his quick temper. He was often the target of abuse by opposing players and fans. Sometimes he would lose his composure, leading him to lash out against those who taunted him. Beckham's temper was a flaw that Ferguson noticed, and it would one day come back to haunt the player.

"Top players will always get [abuse], but they grow up at Manchester United understanding that it's the price they may have to pay for playing at this club," Ferguson said. "The entire team gets [abuse], but some players take more than others and David is under the spotlight now. He is getting quite a bit of abuse, but he just has to handle it like Ryan Giggs has and like [former players] Mark Hughes and Eric Cantona did when they were with us."[6]

Although Ferguson did not address Beckham about his temper, Hoddle did after a series of events involving the player. In a United game against West Ham, the fans hurled obscene chants at Beckham. After he assisted Roy Keane's goal to tie the game at 1–1, Beckham raced toward those fans mouthing insults and waving his arms.

In a United game against Everton, he was again the subject of abuse from the crowd. He responded once again. After heading in a goal to put United in

DID YOU KNOW?

When Beckham first started playing for Manchester United, he wore the number ten jersey. But when Eric Cantona retired in May 1997, he left behind the number seven jersey. With Teddy Sheringham joining United from Tottenham Hotspur, Beckham allowed Sheringham to take the number ten jersey and claimed the number seven jersey for himself. In soccer, the star player traditionally wears the number ten while the right midfielder often wears number seven.

Beckham has always been intense on the soccer field, even in MLS.

front, Beckham taunted Everton fans by putting his hand to his ear, as if he could not hear them.

Later, Beckham was given two yellow cards in a national team game and had to sit out the next match. Hoddle decided it was time to put the clamps on Beckham's temper. In front of the whole team, Hoddle showed a video of Beckham receiving the

HE SAID IT

"Shopping."

—*Beckham's response when asked about one of his strengths*

yellow cards, embarrassing Beckham in front of his teammates.

"I showed it in front of everyone in the squad so that it would sink in," Hoddle said. "David couldn't see it in his own eyes at the time and although his record isn't that bad, the signs were there and it was important to stamp down on it early for him to progress.

"I'm not talking about talent or football ability, just character and temperament. He gets caught in situations he doesn't need to. It's not a youth thing— you don't see Gary and Phil Neville doing it—and it might hold him back in the long run. It's not a major problem but it could be somewhere down the line."[7]

The video seemed to have the desired effect. Beckham realized his actions were childish and not in the best interest of his team. As World Cup qualifying progressed, he was able to keep his temper in check. But whether Beckham and the rest of his

Beckham and England play Italy in a 1997 World Cup qualifier.

EARNING AN AWARD

In 1997, Beckham helped lead Manchester United to the English Premier League title and reach the semifinals of the Champions League. After the season, he was voted Sky Sports/Panasonic Young Player of the Year.

England teammates would get a chance to play in the thirty-two team World Cup finals in France was undecided until the final game of qualification.

In its final game, England traveled to Rome, where the Italians were riding a fifteen-game winning streak. A win or tie would earn England an automatic bid into the World Cup. A loss would force the club to play a home-and-home playoff against another third-place team from a different group. In a tense game, Beckham was able to maintain his composure and help England come away with a 0–0 draw.

England was on its way to the World Cup in France, where the entire world would watch Beckham and his teammates take on national teams from around the globe. "It was an unbelievable experience, a great experience," Beckham said after the tie against Italy. "It's a dream come true for me."[8]

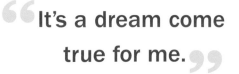

It's a dream come true for me.

—*David Beckham*

FROM HERO
TO GOAT

n the summer of 1998, the eyes of the world
were on France as the World Cup finals were set
to begin. Thanks in large part to David Beckham,
England was in the final field of thirty-two teams. An
entire nation was holding its breath as England
attempted to win its first World Cup since 1966.

As England's first game against Tunisia
approached, most people thought Beckham would
assume his place in the starting eleven. Surprisingly,
the Manchester United star started on the bench.
Hoddle's decision to not start Beckham, or seven-
teen-year-old sensation Michael Owen, worked out
as the English won 2–0. However, Hoddle faced
criticism for this decision and for then having
Beckham address the media after the game. Two of

those firing the criticism were Sir Alex Ferguson and Sir Bobby Charlton.

"Alex Ferguson has already said that he was a little disappointed that Glenn Hoddle put him in front of his press corps, and I agree with that," said Charlton, the English football legend. "David Beckham wants to be the best player in the world. He just knows he has so much skill and ability and I don't think he understands why he's not playing.

"I think he has an ability which isn't anywhere else in the team. His passing and ability to score goals, the quality of his crossing if he plays on the right side. I think you're looking at one of the rare players in the world. He's got fantastic ability."[1]

Hoddle did not listen to Charlton or anyone else when it came to Beckham. When the second game against Romania started, both Beckham and Owen were again on the bench. It was an odd move considering how important Beckham had been for England during qualification. Beckham finally took the field in the thirty-second minute when a team-mate suffered an injury.

The game remained scoreless into the second half until Romania scored a goal. Romania held onto the lead and remained in control of the game until the seventy-second minute, when Hoddle inserted Owen into the lineup. As the game was nearing the end, Beckham crossed the ball into the box. Alan Shearer pulled in the pass and slotted it over to Owen.

The young forward blasted the ball into the back of the net.

England had seemingly avoided disaster with the goal and Beckham was again poised to be a hero. But in stoppage time, Romania stunned the English with another goal to claim the win. With the loss, England had to tie or beat Columbia to qualify for the knock-out phase of the tournament.

Realizing he needed Beckham on the field, Hoddle inserted the midfielder into the starting lineup against Columbia. The move did not pay off immediately as Columbia scored the first goal. But Beckham responded by deftly lifting a free kick past the goalie to give England a 1–1 draw. The result allowed England to advance to the next round as the second-place team from Group G. Back home, Beckham was being hailed as a hero, the young man who kept England's hopes of a World Cup title alive.

QUICK TEMPER DOOMS BECKHAM

Up next for England was Argentina. The South American team was one of the top teams in the world and a favorite to win the World Cup. England would need a strong effort from everyone to win. The

DID YOU KNOW?

Beckham's goal against Colombia in the opening round of the World Cup finals in France was his first goal for the English national team.

Beckham celebrates after his goal against Colombia in the 1998 World Cup.

match got off to a bad start for England when Argentina scored an early goal to claim a 1–0 lead. But England stormed back with 2 goals. The second goal came on a beautifully placed pass from Beckham to Owen. It sent the English fans into a wild celebration.

Argentina, however, was able to even the score at 2–2 before halftime when Javier Zanetti slipped the ball past England's goalie. Any momentum England had was gone. Any chance of reclaiming it vanished minutes into the second half when Argentina midfielder Diego Simeone took Beckham down with a hard tackle. Beckham could have ignored Simeone's attempt to provoke him. Instead, Beckham lashed back by kicking Simeone right in front of the referee. The referee immediately gave Beckham a red card, meaning he was ejected from the game and England was not allowed to replace him. England would have to play the rest of the match with one less player than Argentina.

The fear that Beckham's temper would come back to cost him and his team had come true—and at the worst time possible. "I have tried to ram it home to him that it's a physical game where players of talent will always be singled out for a hard time," Ferguson

WRONG TIME FOR A FIRST

The red card Beckham was shown against Argentina in the 1998 World Cup was the first of his career.

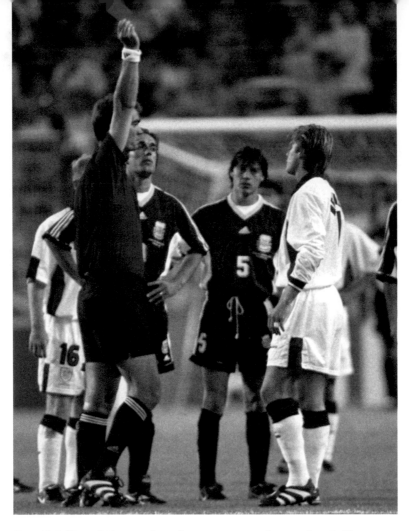

David Beckham is shown a red card at the 1998 World Cup.

said about the incident. "I have told him that the only way to get back at opponents who do that is by showing he is better with the ball than they are. But in the heat of the contest he doesn't always keep control."[2]

Playing with a man down, England put on a valiant effort. The team thought it had taken the lead when Sol Campbell scored on a header. But the goal was disallowed because an English player had committed a foul before the goal. The game ended in a 2–2 draw after regulation and extra time, forcing the contest to be settled on penalty kicks. Argentina edged England 4–3 to eliminate England from the World Cup.

> **"I have tried to ram it home to him that it's a physical game where players of talent will always be singled out for a hard time. "**
>
> —*Sir Alex Ferguson*

As soon as the match was over, fans around England blamed Beckham for the loss. Hoddle did his best to try to deflect some of the anger directed at his ejected player. "David Beckham's sending off cost us dearly," Hoddle said. "I am not denying it cost us the game. But it would be wrong to put the blame on David Beckham's shoulders or anybody's shoulders. I'm not looking for someone to blame. I just hope that the country next year respect[s] the fact that he has done fantastic in the past. And he has got a great, great future—[if we let him go,] we would be cutting our noses off to spite our face."[3]

Meanwhile, Beckham was at the lowest point in his career. He knew he had made a mistake the instant he let his temper get the better of him, and he apologized to everyone about his behavior on

1998 WORLD CUP

Host: France
Champion: France
Runner-up: Brazil
Third: Croatia
Golden Boot: Davor Suker, Croatia, with 6 goals

the field. "This is without doubt the worst moment of my career," Beckham said. "I will always regret my actions. I have apologized to the England players and management and I want every England supporter to know how deeply sorry I am."[4]

He continued: "I stood in the tunnel and watched the last few minutes and the terrible tension of the penalty shootout. That was worse than anything else. It was then I fully realized what I had done. I kept thinking to myself that, if I had been out there, I would have been one of the penalty kickers. The rest of them had done so much without me and I had let them down desperately."[5]

Charlton did his best to help calm the upset England supporters. "You cannot throw him to the wolves," Charlton said. "I saw him after the match and he was terribly affected by it. He realized what he had done. He is a young man who was very much affected by it, I know that, and he will have other World Cups where he can put that right."[6]

England fans were not in the mood to listen to Charlton or anyone else defending Beckham. One fan from North London said that next Beckham should put a skirt on and join the Spice Girls, a reference to Beckham's then girlfriend, Victoria "Posh Spice" Adams. Another fan from Suffolk said Beckham let down the entire nation. The tabloids roasted Beckham as well. One local paper ran the headline "Ten Heroic Lions, One Stupid Boy." One of the paper's soccer reporters suggested that Beckham not be allowed back on the national team ever again.

Another newspaper printed a dartboard with Beckham's face on it and a radio station ran a poll that resulted in sixty-one percent of the listeners saying they never wanted to see Beckham on the national team again. He even received some death threats. The constant barrage of insults and mean-spirited articles was all due to one mistake. It was enough to disgust Ferguson.

"What David did was foolish and unprofessional," Ferguson said. "He has to live with the

HE SAID IT

"This is without doubt the worst moment of my career. I will always regret my actions during last night's game."
—Beckham on how he felt after being ejected from a 1998 World Cup match against Argentina

damage his action did to England's chances of reaching the quarterfinals of the World Cup. But I was sickened by much of the cruel nonsense produced about Beckham last week."[7]

The hatred toward Beckham affected him greatly. Ted Beckham said his son was not talking about the sport he had loved his whole life. He said Beckham was even worried about returning to training with Manchester United for the start of the season. Beckham finally fled to the United States, where he was still relatively unknown and so out of the public eye.

Beckham eventually returned from the United States and reported to Manchester United for training ahead of the 1998–99 season. At this point, Ferguson publicly offered his support to Beckham, saying the team would look after him and protect him. Beckham was appreciative of Ferguson's gesture. "Knowing he was behind me really helped me get through that summer in 1998 and the early part of the season that followed," Beckham said.[8]

The support Beckham received from his manager and United fans proved to be valuable. It allowed him to turn the page on the events in France. And it allowed him to once again become a hero in England.

REDEMPTION

The red card in France could have been the prelude to the end of David Beckham's career, at least on the national team and in the English Premier League. No matter where he went the following season, that one event plagued him as opposing fans taunted him whenever possible. It would have been easy for Beckham to give in and ask for a transfer to a club outside England.

Instead, Beckham showed his mental strength by pushing all of the insults aside. He focused on what he had to do on the field to help Manchester United win. His desire to prove others wrong pushed him to have one of the best stretches of his career and lead the Red Devils to one of their greatest seasons ever.

As the season progressed, Manchester United established itself as not just one of the best clubs in England, but in all of Europe. Domestically, United was at the top of the EPL standings and was determined to reclaim the league title that Arsenal had won the previous season.

In the FA Cup, one of the oldest and most original tournaments in the world, hundreds of soccer teams from all levels in England competed for the title. Just as in league play, Manchester United was rolling through the FA Cup. The same was holding true in the Champions League.

The Red Devils were nearly unstoppable. Entering the final month of the season, United had a realistic shot of earning the "treble," which means winning three titles in one season. The team would have to win the EPL, FA Cup, and Champions League.

Beckham scored 8 goals for United that season, a high total considering he was a midfielder. Two of those goals came in two of the Red Devils' most important matches. In the FA Cup semifinals against Arsenal, Beckham pounced on a loose ball in Arsenal's penalty area and blasted it past goalie David Seaman. The goal proved crucial. Arsenal scored a late goal to even the match. However, Manchester United scored in extra time to advance to the FA Cup final. It went on to defeat Newcastle 2–0 to claim the FA Cup title.

Beckham celebrates after a goal against Arsenal in the 1999 FA Cup semifinals.

In the EPL season finale against Tottenham Hotspur, the team that had tried so hard to land Beckham at the start of his career, Beckham scored a first-half goal to help lead the Red Devils to a 2–1 victory and the league title.

Although Beckham was scoring more, his passing and free kicks were still as good as ever. In a

Champions League quarterfinal match, Beckham set up 2 goals for Dwight Yorke in a 2–0 victory.

In the second game of a semifinal series against Juventus, a team from Italy, Manchester United trailed 2–0 after only ten minutes. The teams had tied 1–1 in the first match at Old Trafford in Manchester. United needed a spark, and Beckham came through. On a corner kick, Beckham lifted the ball toward the goal. Roy Keane redirected the ball into the goal with his head. Given new life, the Red Devils tied the contest on a Yorke goal and the teams were tied at the half. Andy Cole then scored in the second half to secure the 3–2 triumph for Manchester United and a trip to the Champions League final.

A FINISH TO REMEMBER

The final of the Champions League featured Manchester United against Bayern Munich of Germany. Entering the match, key United midfielders Keane and Paul Scholes had been suspended due to an accumulation of yellow cards. Ferguson was forced to change his lineup and move some people around. The United players came out flat and played one of their worst games of the season. The Red Devils trailed 1–0 as the match went into injury time. The team needed something miraculous to happen if they wanted to win the treble.

An offense that had been dormant all game suddenly came to life. With only three minutes expected for injury time, United attacked the Bayern Munich goal and earned a corner kick. Beckham swung the ball in and it fell to midfielder Ryan Giggs. His shot appeared to be going wide. Seemingly out of nowhere, Teddy Sheringham was in the path of the ball and directed it into the goal. The game was tied 1–1.

The crowd went wild and believed the contest was headed into overtime. But United did not want that. The team had the momentum and continued its attacking style. Ole Gunnar Solskjaer, who came into the game as a substitute for Manchester United, earned the Red Devils a corner kick. Everyone knew what that meant.

Beckham ran to the corner to place the ball. Rising as one, the 90,000 people in attendance watched Beckham boot the ball and swing it in toward the goal. Sheringham jumped high into the air and headed the ball down into the six-yard box. Somehow, the ball found Solskjaer, who was unmarked by the defense. He flicked his right foot and sent the ball into the net to score one of the most famous goals in Manchester United history.

In a matter of minutes, Beckham and his teammates had turned sure defeat into a stunning victory, earning the club the treble. For Beckham, the win capped a comeback season. While not a national hero yet, he was no longer the national villain.

Beckham and his Manchester United teammates celebrate their English Premier League title in 1999.

MEETING THE GIRL OF HIS DREAMS

In 1996, when Beckham was twenty-two, he was on a trip with the English national team. During some down time, Beckham was watching television when a Spice Girls music video came on. Pointing at the screen, he turned to friend and teammate Gary Neville and said that Victoria Adams, known as Posh Spice with the group, was the woman he wanted and that they would be together forever. Soon, the two were dating and quickly became one of the most talked about couples in England. Less than three years later, on July 4, 1999, the two were married. The couple's first son Brooklyn, who was four months old at the time, was the ring bearer at the wedding.

AN IMPORTANT PHONE CALL

Manchester United added another EPL title the following season, but it did not repeat its treble. The Red Devils lost to Real Madrid in the quarterfinals of the Champions League and did not compete

GOOD THING THEY WEREN'T IN PITTSBURGH

Beckham and his wife, Victoria, chose the name "Brooklyn" for their oldest son because they were in Brooklyn, New York, when they found out Victoria was pregnant.

DID YOU KNOW?

Gary Neville, who played with Beckham on the Manchester United youth team as well as the senior team, was the best man at Beckham's wedding.

in the FA Cup due to their participation in the World Club Championship, which is now called the Club World Cup.

In the fall of 2000, Beckham received a phone call he probably thought would never come after what had happened in 1998. On the phone was interim national team coach Peter Taylor. "Sorry to ring this early but I'm about to announce the squad," Taylor said to Beckham at 8:00 a.m. "I've picked a young group and some new players. I think the right thing is for you to captain them. I've got absolutely no doubt about you being ready for the job."[1]

Beckham was stunned by the news. Being named captain of a team is a great honor, so to be the captain of the national team is an amazing accomplishment. The red card in France was now a distant memory. In just two years, Beckham helped lead Manchester United to unprecedented heights and reestablish himself as one of the most popular players in England. "Two years ago if someone had turned around and said 'in two years time you'll be England captain,' I'd have said 'I don't think so,'" Beckham said.[2]

ANOTHER TITLE, ANOTHER COACH
In 2001, Manchester United claimed its sixth EPL title in seven years and seventh in nine years. Every-thing was going well for Beckham, even on the national team. Sven-Goran Ericksson had taken over as manager of the team. He may have had another choice for leader on the field, but he decided to keep Beckham as the captain. "I think you'll make a great England captain," Ericksson said. "You're a good enough player and a player others can look up to. Anybody who doubts that, it's your job to prove then wrong."[3]

As 2001 progressed, England played a series of World Cup qualifying games for the 2002 World Cup in South Korea and Japan. As in 1998, England's chances of advancing hinged on what it would do in its final game of round-robin group play. Facing Greece, England once again needed a tie to advance. But Greece was on the verge of sending England home as it held a 2–1 lead late in the match. Beck-ham's right foot made sure England would survive.

Late in the contest, England was awarded a free kick nearly twenty-five yards from the goal. Beckham calmly stood over the ball. Throughout the game his passing had been strong, but he was uncharacteristi-cally struggling with his free kicks. "I'd missed a few that afternoon," Beckham said. "But I wasn't going to give this last one up. I knew this was our last chance."[4]

The sellout crowd of more than 66,000 fans anxiously watched. Beckham approached the ball and struck it perfectly with his right foot, sending the ball over the wall of defenders and into the upper corner of the net. The crowed went wild and the English players embraced Beckham. "The moment I made contact, I knew this one was in," Beckham said.[5]

Ericksson said it was Beckham's determination that helped England salvage the tie. "You could see he wanted really hard to win this and he showed again he is a really great captain," he said.[6]

> **"The moment I made contact, I knew this one was in.**
>
> —David Beckham

BECKS THE HERO

"If you're that good a player you'll always come out at the end of the day as the hero. You always know what a world-class player he is and that one of these days he was going to take us to, or maybe even win us, a World Cup."

—Teammate Michael Owen on Beckham after the win over Greece

⭐ MEMORABLE GAME

Beckham earned his 50th cap, or appearance, for England on June 2, 2002 in the opening game of the World Cup finals against Sweden.

DEALT ANOTHER BLOW

The fans carried the excitement of heading to the World Cup finals into 2002. But that euphoria suddenly came crashing down when Beckham suffered an injury to his left foot in a Champions League game against Deportivo la Coruna of Spain. X-rays showed the captain had a fractured bone in his foot and he would be out for at least eight weeks. The diagnosis was then reduced to six weeks, but there was still doubt about Beckham being healed in time for the World Cup.

Fate must have been on Beckham's side. The broken bone healed quickly enough that Beckham headed to Asia with his teammates. While there, he would bury the demons of 1998 once and for all. In the opener against Sweden, Beckham set up a goal on a corner kick to help England earn a 1–1 draw. Then came a match against Argentina, the team that had ousted England from the 1998 World Cup.

All the memories of that fateful day in France came back. Beckham's red card was discussed day after day. On the field once again for Argentina was Diego Simeone. This time, he would not be able to provoke Beckham. Instead, the captain of the English squad spent the match barking orders to his teammates and making sure they were in the right alignment. The game was physical, as it always seemed to be when the two teams faced each other. Late in the first half, Argentina was called for a foul in its own penalty box, giving England a penalty kick.

There was no question about who was going to take the shot. Beckham confidently placed the ball on the ground. When the referee blew the whistle, Beckham approached the ball and rocketed it into the back of the net. Just like that, Beckham had redeemed himself once and for all. England won 1–0. He was again a hero in England.

"For me, it was the best and biggest thing that I could've ever done in my career at that time," Beckham said. "The moment the ball struck the back of the net, funnily enough, my mind went clear,

MEMORABLE GOAL

"It's unbelievable. It's been four years. It's been a long four years."

—Beckham, after scoring the goal that helped beat Argentina in the 2002 World Cup

HAIRSTYLE

The always-stylish Beckham made headlines at the 2002 World Cup not only for his play but also for his hair. Beckham sported a variation of a Mohawk in which his hair was cut short on the side with longer, bleached hair pushed together to form a line on the top. This style, sometimes called a "fauxhawk," grew in popularity after Beckham sported it in 2002.

everything that I was thinking, everything that I had gone through. I knew how much it meant for me to score that goal for my family and, of course, for the fans, because the rivalry against Argentina is huge."[7]

England finished second in their group to advance to the round of sixteen. After a 3–0 win against Denmark, England lost 2–1 to eventual champion Brazil in the quarterfinals.

Beckham makes a penalty kick against Argentina in the 2002 World Cup.

OFF TO SPAIN

David Beckham was still playing at a high level on the field, but his relationship with Sir Alex Ferguson had slowly been eroding. Ferguson disapproved of Beckham's behavior, though not on the soccer field. He believed that Beckham's lavish lifestyle with his wife, Victoria Adams, the former Posh Spice, was affecting his preparation for games.

Beckham said rumors he and Ferguson did not like each other were false. "Despite what many people say about me and Sir Alex Ferguson, he's been a father figure to me," Beckham said.[1]

But the father-son relationship they had enjoyed was not as strong as it had once been. During the 2002–03 season, Manchester United suffered a 2–0 loss to Arsenal in the fifth round of the FA Cup. After the match, an upset Ferguson kicked a shoe that struck Beckham in the face. The gash needed stitches to close. The relationship between the two men changed after that. Manchester United won fifteen of its final eighteen matches that season to win the EPL title once again, but Beckham was benched for several of those games. It was becoming apparent that his time at Manchester United was coming to an end.

THE ROAD TO REAL MADRID

During the offseason, Manchester United agreed to sell the rights to Beckham to Spanish soccer power FC Barcelona. Beckham, however, had to agree to the deal, and he did not want to join Barcelona. Beckham, who was in the United States when the agreement was announced, was also upset that Manchester United had not approached him first.

Barcelona was never able to reach an agreement with Beckham, but the midfielder was clearly on his way out of Manchester. Several teams were still showing an interest in acquiring Beckham, including giants AC Milan, Internazionale of Milan, and Real Madrid.

UNFULFILLED PROMISE

Joan Laporta, a candidate in the FC Barcelona presidential election, told fans he would bring Beckham to Barcelona if he won. Laporta won, but Beckham did not come to Barcelona.

One week after Barcelona's failed attempt to land Beckham, now twenty-eight, Manchester United agreed to sell him to Real Madrid. The club confirmed the deal on June 18, which was to be completed in July.

Although most people knew Beckham's run with the Red Devils was coming to an end, it was still hard for them to let the superstar leave. One such person was Ferguson, the team's longtime manager. "I've known David since he was eleven years of age, and it's been a pleasure to see him grow and develop into the player he has become," he said. "David has been an integral part of all the successes that Manchester United [has] achieved in the last decade. I would like to wish him and his family every success in the future, and thank him for his service to the club."[2]

Said Beckham about his departure from Manchester United: "I will always hold precious memories of my time at Manchester United and Old Trafford as well as the players, who I regard as part of

HE SAID IT

"Playing for a club like Madrid improves everyone. Whatever the player or how big a name you are, if you don't perform you don't play."

—David Beckham on playing for Real Madrid

my family, and the brilliant fans who have given me so much support over the years and continue to do so."[3]

Just like his eventual move to Los Angeles, Beckham's transfer to Real Madrid was worldwide news. At his official unveiling in Madrid, a huge throng of fans showed up and more than five hundred journalists from twenty-five countries covered the event. Beckham was handed a jersey with the number twenty-three on the back, a number made famous in America by basketball star Michael Jordan, whom Beckham admired. The number had also been made famous in Madrid by Argentina legend Alfredo di Stefano, who wore it for Real Madrid in the 1950s and 1960s.

As always, Beckham was humble during the news conference, speaking in his famous soft voice. "I have always loved football," Beckham said. "Of course I love my family. I have a wonderful life, but football is everything to me and joining Real Madrid is a dream come true. I would like to say thank you to everyone coming and joining me in my arrival. *Gracias—hala Madrid!*"[4]

Real Madrid already had a stable of superstars. On the roster were world-class players such as Zinedine Zidane of France, Raúl of Spain, Brazilians Ronaldo and Roberto Carlos, and Luis Figo of Portugal. Madrid president Florentino Perez, however, made sure everyone knew that, with Beckham, Real Madrid was adding another great player. "Despite all

Beckham makes his Madrid debut in style.

that's going on, we're not going to lose sight of the fact that we are unveiling this great player," Perez said. "He is a great player who is going to become part of the club's great history. He is a man of our times and a symbol of modern-day stardom and what is certain is Real [has] signed Beckham because he's a great footballer and a very dedicated professional."[5]

The Real Madrid fans quickly embraced Beckham. His jersey was the top seller among all of the players' jerseys in the team's store. When the season started, the fans wanted Beckham to take free kicks and corners. Roberto Carlos had customarily taken those kicks for Real Madrid in past seasons.

There is an adjustment period whenever a player switches teams. For Beckham, that adjustment could have been tough. The styles of play between the English Premier League and the Spanish La Liga are very different. Throw in the cultural differences between Manchester and Madrid and the huge expectations of the Real Madrid fans, and Beckham could have been lost on the field. Instead, he quickly embraced his new surroundings.

"I think, in the beginning, he was under pressure because people expected a little bit more," Figo said. "I think he . . . is doing a great job for Real Madrid. He is a really important player for us and has made us even stronger this year.

"I don't know how much he has improved but [it] is always good for a player to come into contact

HE SAID IT

"In Spain people have lunch and dinner a lot later—when I return to England I'll have to eat alone at midnight."
—David Beckham, remarking on a Spanish custom. It's not an exaggeration that, in Spain, dinner often starts as late as midnight.

Five of Real Madrid's Galacticos in 2004: Beckham,
Luis Figo, Ronaldo, Zinedine Zidane, and Raúl.

with the very best players [and] he is playing with
Zinedine Zidane, Ronaldo, Raúl, and Roberto
Carlos."[6]

IN SEARCH OF SUCCESS

Real Madrid won a lot of games, but it was unable
to win the La Liga title, Spain's Copa del Rey

tournament (similar to England's FA Cup), or the Champions League during Beckham's first three seasons with the team. Fans were disappointed.

On England's national team, Beckham and his teammates remained unlucky as well. At the 2004 European Championships in Portugal, a competition pitting the top national teams in Europe against each other, England started well and advanced to the quarterfinals. England and host Portugal played to a 2–2 draw and the match had to be decided by penalty kicks. Beckham lined up to take the first kick for England. He planted his left foot and struck the ball. But his left foot slipped forward and the ball sailed high over the goal and into the crowd. Portugal went on to defeat England 6–5 in sudden death.

Unlike in 1998, Beckham avoided blame for the loss. But he still felt bad about the miss, knowing how much the English fans want to win a World Cup or European championship. In Germany, at the 2006 World Cup, Beckham again had an outstanding performance throughout the tournament.

Playing Ecuador on a hot, muggy day, Beckham lifted the spirits of the team and fans when he performed his signature skill. He curled a twenty-five yard free kick inside the post of the goal in the sixtieth minute to lead England to a 1–0 victory. That goal made Beckham the first English player to score in three World Cup finals tournaments. Unfortunately, Beckham's magical right foot would not be able to lead England to the championship. Just as it did during the European Championships, Portugal beat England to eliminate them from the event.

RUN AT REAL COMING TO AN END

Months later, rumors started to circulate that Beckham would leave Real Madrid for the United States to play in Major League Soccer. His deal with Real Madrid was set to end in June 2007, and so Beckham was allowed to start negotiating with other clubs. Real Madrid wanted Beckham to come to a decision as soon as possible.

Real Madrid was interested in having the star return to the team. This was despite the fact that manager Fabio Capello was keeping Beckham on the bench for several matches early in the 2007–08 season. Beckham was mainly being used as a substitute. With his future uncertain, teams from England, France, Italy, Spain, and the United States were interested in adding Beckham to their squads. As time passed, Real Madrid was becoming more insistent that Beckham make up his mind about his future.

In January 2007, the club made up Beckham's mind for him. Real Madrid's sporting director Predrag Mijatovic said Beckham would not return to Real Madrid at the end of the season. Mijatovic later said he had been misunderstood and had said only that the player's contract with the team had not been renewed at that time. But by then it did not

ANOTHER BOY

In September 2002, David and Victoria Beckham welcomed Romeo, their second son, into their family.

matter what he said. Beckham announced his five-year deal with the Los Angeles Galaxy the next day.

The announcement made Capello angry. The manager announced that Beckham had played his last game in a Real Madrid uniform, even though half the season was yet to be played. Beckham was stunned by Capello's reaction. It was not unusual for players to announce a future deal with a different club. But instead of lashing out, Beckham maintained his professionalism and continued to train hard, despite knowing he would not play in a game.

Capello soon realized he had made a mistake in banishing Beckham and allowed him to rejoin the lineup. Beckham was eager to play and scored in his first match back. It was a victory that sparked a magical finish for Real and Beckham.

With Beckham back on the field, Real Madrid defeated Bayern Munich 3–2 in the Champions League as Beckham had 2 assists. In La Liga play, Real Madrid chased down leader FC Barcelona to set up a win-or-else season finale against Mallorca.

Beckham with his kids (from left) Brooklyn, Cruz, and Romeo after winning the 2007 Spanish La Liga title.

Barcelona and Real Madrid entered the final game tied for first place. Real, however, owned the tiebreaker because of its 1–0–1 record against Barcelona. While Real was facing Mallorca, Barcelona easily defeated Gimnastic 5–1. After this game, Real Madrid knew it had to win or else lose the league title to archrival Barcelona.

Hobbled by a left ankle injury, Beckham did all he could to lead his team on the field. One of his shots sailed just over the crossbar, landing on the roof of the net. A second shot clanged off the crossbar.

Eventually, with his left ankle throbbing, Beckham left the field to be replaced by Jose Antonio Reyes in the sixty-sixth minute with Real trailing 1–0.

Reyes was the spark Real needed. He scored two minutes later to even the score. Real Madrid scored once again with nine minutes remaining, and Reyes scored two minutes after that to lift the club to a 3–1 victory and the La Liga title. For Beckham, it was a magical way to end his career at Real Madrid. He finally was able to win the elusive title the club had sought since he had joined the team in 2003.

> **"I was wrong about two things this season. Firstly, not renewing Beckham's contract. Secondly, keeping him apart from the team."**
>
> —*Fabio Capello*

After the match, Capello admitted he had made a mistake when it came to Beckham that season. "I was wrong about two things this season," Capello said. "Firstly, not renewing Beckham's contract. Secondly, keeping him apart from the team."[7]

But Capello's realization came too late. Beckham was no longer a member of Real Madrid. In fact, he was only weeks away from his debut in the United States for the Galaxy.

WORLD ICON

David Beckham's exploits on the field have always been well chronicled. But his exploits off the field might be just as well documented. Fans on all continents scream his name and plead for an autograph or a picture.

Beckham does not get much time alone, especially when he is out in public. But that is fine with him. "I enjoy all the attention. Who wouldn't?" he said. "It doesn't bother me. I was like that once. I was a little kid who wanted autographs of older players and those I admired. I respect that and I've loads of time for supporters. If you are in the public eye it's something you must put up with.

"If you go out for a quiet meal in the afternoon and get photographed, it's one of those things. . . . Most of the time it's fine by me. Sometimes I think it's unfair on the person you're with, but they also expect it."[1]

BECKS AND POSH

He was a superstar soccer player, adored by fans as much for his talent as for his looks. She was an attractive superstar pop singer. Once Beckham and Victoria Adams became a couple in 1997, it was a rare day when a tabloid did not run a photo or a story about the two. Again, Beckham just shrugged off the attention. "I'm a footballer and she's a Spice Girl. It'd be silly if we did not think the media and the public were attracted to us. But we are just two normal young people going out together," he said. "It helps that Victoria is famous. It helps with the pressure if she is involved because we both share it.

FAME'S DRAWBACKS

Beckham and his wife are one of the most famous couples in the world, but are especially celebrated in England. Seldom can the two go anywhere without having people taking pictures and following them. At times, Beckham's fame becomes overwhelming.

"At home things are hard," he said. "For instance, my curtains are never open. I get no privacy at all. In fact, I can't remember the last time I saw daylight in my house."

Beckham and future wife Victoria in 1998

I don't see myself as front-page material, but going out with Victoria I am going to get it. We realize it is something we must handle."[2]

As the courtship continued, Beckham introduced Adams to his family. She was welcomed with open arms, but Ted Beckham was somewhat worried about the consequences of his son dating a pop star, especially while she was at the height of her popularity.

"You're very wary of anyone getting together . . . [in] the pop star world," Ted Beckham said. "We were worried. I like David going to bed at 10:00 p.m. purely because he's a disciplined professional football player. David's not a drinker, he's never been a drinker. The pop world . . . you don't know what time they're out until. That was our worry. At the end of the day, it's David's wishes. If he wants to go out with Victoria, that's down to David. It's not down to us."[3]

In 1999, Beckham and Adams got married in one of the most lavish events of the year. At the wedding dinner, the couple sat on golden thrones and Adams wore a crown, living up to her Posh Spice image. The ceremony was held in a castle outside of Dublin, Ireland. Although they invited only twenty-nine guests, the event cost more than $700,000!

HE SAID IT

"I've got more clothes than Victoria."
—*David Beckham, comparing the size of his wardrobe to his wife's*

Since the wedding, the Beckhams have had two more children to join Brooklyn: Romeo and Cruz. The birth of each child was national news, thrusting the family even more into the spotlight. Beckham is so famous, even his father admits he is somewhat in awe of his son.

> 66 **Believe it or not, I do get star-struck by my own son.** 99
>
> *—Ted Beckham*

"Believe it or not, I do get star-struck by my own son," Ted said. "It's a weird feeling. You think, 'Oh it's my son,' and then you think, 'He's a superstar!'"[4]

JUST A FAMILY MAN

Despite being in the public eye, Beckham does everything possible to be with Victoria and his three sons. According to Ted, Beckham has done a great

A GIRL'S NAME

Beckham and his wife Victoria named their third son Cruz. He was born in Madrid, Spain, in February 2005. Some people criticized the name because, in Spain, Cruz is a female name, and they felt it was inappropriate to give it to a boy.

job as a father. "David is a brilliant dad. He's unbelievable," Ted said. "With all his babies, he would take them out and change them. Unfortunately, he's away a lot with his football but tries to do as much with Brooklyn, Romeo, and Cruz as he can."[5]

Though Beckham is used to the bright glare of the media and public spotlight, he admits it can become a bit overwhelming. Luckily for him, he still has his soccer career to turn to.

DID YOU KNOW?

In 2001, Beckham was voted the best male body in *Celebrity Bodies* magazine and Best Dressed Male by readers of *Heat* magazine in the United Kingdom.

When he is on the field, Beckham is calm and relaxed. "There is this madness around me, around my family," Beckham said. "Without a doubt, out on the field is where I'm most comfortable, where I'm happiest, because I know what I'm doing, and I know I can do it."[6]

When Beckham has time to be with his family, he and Victoria are like most parents. They spend time with their children and together. While they have a lifestyle not many other couples have, they are, according to friend David Furnish, content to stay home and watch movies.

Soccer legend Pelé (left) and Beckham, two of the most famous athletes of all time, pose in 2008.

MAN OF MANY INTERESTS

The only way to really describe Beckham accurately is to call him an "icon." He is a soccer icon, media icon, business icon, and fashion icon. He has been written about and photographed thousands of times. As a businessman, he has launched his own cologne. And in the fashion world, he has posed for a number of fashion magazines, wearing world-famous designer suits or only a pair of underwear. This has allowed Beckham to build a following of non-soccer fans on par with the number of soccer fans who follow his career. If Beckham changes his hairstyle, his new look is immediately copied by hundreds of thousands of fans. During his career, he has sported many hairstyles, including the fauxhawk look, a ponytail, and dreadlocks. Once, he went with a nearly shaven head.

Beckham was once photographed wearing a sarong, a large scarf tied around the waist like a skirt, while in France when he and Victoria were still only dating. The photos were seen around the world and drew comments from men and women alike. "People seem to be endlessly fascinated with them," Furnish said. "I think it's because David and Victoria represent the dreams of a lot of British people. Every British boy wants to grow up and be a footballer, and every British girl would love to grow up and be a pop star and marry a footballer. . . . They both have this amazing star quality, in addition to being successful at what they do. As a society, we can't seem to get enough of it."[7]

Beckham is not the first athlete to juggle being a

HE SAID IT

"As a footballer you always want to test yourself against the best."

—David Beckham

superstar on the field and an icon off the field. He is, however, one of the few people to be a world icon. "We think that David Beckham is one of the contemporary icons, a reference point, internationally acknowledged by millions of men and woman," said designers Domenico Dolce and Stefano Gabbana. "We are inspired by his positives, by his beauty, for being an excellent athlete."[8]

GIVING BACK

Many athletes around the world get involved with charities and organizations that help those who are less fortunate or in need of aid. David Beckham is no exception.

He has helped create soccer academies in England and in Los Angeles and is planning more in various parts of the world. The goal is to teach the game he loves to as many girls and boys as possible, especially to those who cannot afford to go to soccer camps.

"After football, I've got my academies that I've just started up and I feel very strongly about them," Beckham said. "It's a very personal thing for me that I've always wanted. I'm also a UNICEF ambassador and that's going to be a big part of my life when I finish playing, plus spending time with the kids and my wife Victoria."[1]

In his role as Goodwill Ambassador for the United Nations Children's Fund (UNICEF), one of the first things he helped with was sending needed supplies to the children affected by the tsunami that struck Asia in 2004. "I, like any other person, was deeply moved by the effects of the tsunami disaster," Beckham said while visiting UNICEF's Supply Division in Copenhagen, Denmark. "So many people have lost loved ones and particularly children have suffered greatly with over a million who are vulnerable and at risk of disease.

"People have been so generous to date and it is important that they continue to donate money to organizations such as UNICEF to help in aid relief and reconstruction. It is one of the proudest moments of

NOW THAT'S A PARTY!

In an attempt to raise money for UNICEF, Beckham and his wife Victoria invited friends to a "Full Length and Fabulous" charity party. The event raised more than $2 million. Guests bid on items ranging from a trip to New York to spend a weekend at rapper Sean "Diddy" Combs's apartment to a meal cooked by former rock star Ozzy Osbourne.

DID YOU KNOW?

U2 lead singer Bono asked Beckham to climb one of the world's highest mountains, Mount Kilimanjaro in Africa, for charity and Beckham said yes. No date has been determined yet as to when he will attempt the climb, but it is a challenge Beckham looks forward to.

my life to be given the role of UNICEF Goodwill Ambassador and I hope to play a part in supporting these children at their time of need."[2]

Beckham is also a spokesman for Malaria No More, a non-profit that works to prevent the deadly disease caused by mosquito bites, and supports Help for Heroes, a charity aimed at helping injured service personnel returning from Iraq and Afghanistan. His own charity, the Victoria and David Beckham Charitable Trust, provides wheelchairs to children in need.

During a break in his schedule, he traveled to Sierra Leone in January 2007 to help the fight against AIDS and poverty that afflicts so many children throughout Africa. "We can't turn a blind eye to the tens of thousands of young children who die every day in the developing world, mostly from causes that are preventable," Beckham said. "In Sierra Leone, one in four children dies before reaching their fifth birthday—it's shocking and tragic especially when the

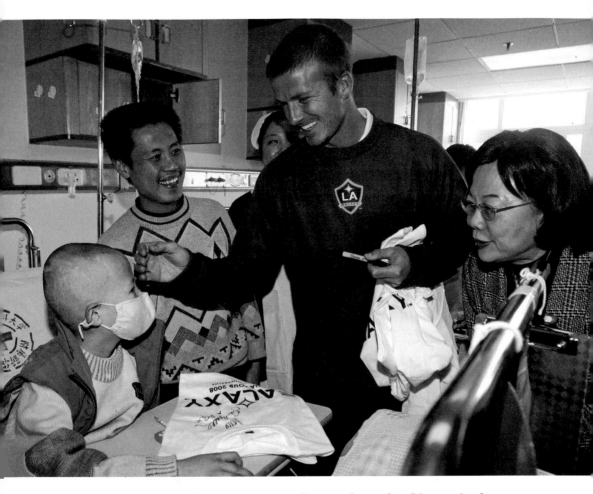

Beckham visits with a leukemia patient in Shanghai, China, in 2008.

solutions are simple—things like vaccinations against measles or using a mosquito net to reduce the chance of getting malaria. Saving these children's lives is a top priority for UNICEF and as an ambassador I hope I can help to draw attention to this issue across the world."[3]

LONDON'S OLYMPIC DREAMS

Beckham played a prominent role in helping London win the bid for the 2012 Olympics. The London Olympic Committee asked Beckham to get involved in the bidding process, and he quickly accepted. Beckham even traveled to Singapore for the final decision.

HELPING ON A PERSONAL LEVEL

In 2006, Beckham's charity helped a young boy named Ollie Rycraft, who was battling his fourth brain tumor and had been left needing a wheelchair. One day, Ollie's mother, Debbie, received a call from Victoria's mother, Jackie Adams. "When she said that David and Victoria would like to buy Ollie the wheelchair I burst into floods of tears," Debbie said. "At first I thought it was a joke but then when the news sunk in I just sobbed 'thank you' down the phone."[4]

The Beckhams had learned of Ollie's condition when one of his physiotherapists, Kate Mills, wrote a letter to the couple. Only a few weeks later, a wheelchair was on the way. "I couldn't wait to get my hands on the wheelchair because it helps me to get around and be independent," Ollie said. "I might be a Chelsea fan but I think David Beckham is great and a really good player."[5]

THE ACADEMY

The David Beckham Academy strives to improve the skills of boys and girls who hope to become professional soccer players. In addition to classrooms and training facilities, the latest technology helps the players learn, improve their skills, and have fun.

ALWAYS HELPING THE CHILDREN

Most of the causes Beckham supports concern children, and helping children was the motivation in November 2006 when he made an appearance on the British television program "Blue Peter" to promote his charity "Shoebiz." The goal of the campaign was to collect and recycle 500,000 pairs of shoes that would in turn raise money to set up twenty-two Children's Corners in Malawi.

Children's Corners provide food, support, schooling, and shoes for some of the world's poorest children in Africa. Many of the children are orphans whose parents died of AIDS. Beckham donated a pair of his own shoes as well as those of several teammates and former British Prime Minister Tony Blair.

"So many people look up to me and to other footballers around the world. To help out by creating awareness is the best thing I can do," Beckham said. "My kids love football and they are lucky—there are many children out there who don't have the privilege of running around grass or having shoes to run in.

"Just a simple thing like giving shoes or trainers to this appeal is going to make a difference. There are many children out there who have lost their mums or dads to HIV/AIDS and something like this will make a huge difference."[6]

> **"So many people look up to me and to other footballers around the world. To help out by creating awareness is the best thing I can do."**
>
> —David Beckham

HELPING IN THE UNITED STATES AS WELL

When Beckham arrived in Los Angeles, not only did he bring his soccer skills with him, but his generosity as well. Wild fires ravaged southern California in the fall of 2007, destroying hundreds of homes and affecting thousands of people. In an effort to help the victims of the fires, Beckham helped organize a soccer game featuring the Galaxy against Hollywood celebrities.

Los Angeles defeated "Hollywood United" 12–4. Beckham had 2 goals and 2 assists. More importantly, the game raised $100,000 to aid the victims, while a silent auction helped raise an additional $7,500 for the American Red Cross and Salvation Army. "It's great to play in a game that

raises money for people who need it," Beckham said. "It's special."[7]

Another one of Beckham's causes is lending his support to an anti-knife campaign in England. Beckham experienced firsthand the dangers of knives when he was a teenager. When he was thirteen, the brother of one of his best friends was stabbed in the back after trying to break up a fight. The boy was left paralyzed and his dream of being a professional soccer player came to an end.

"No one wants to see the devastation I saw my friend and his family go through. We have to lend our support to this campaign," Beckham said. "You don't

Beckham poses with young soccer players at one of his youth clinics in Harlem, New York.

95

expect situations that are happening whereby people go to school in the morning and then you never see them again because of incidents that have happened. We have got to help. We have got a voice the kids listen to so it is important we get involved in something like this."[8]

Beckham has made sure he is involved in as many good causes as possible. One day his playing career will be over. But he plans to continue his charitable ways for years to come.

DID YOU KNOW?

Singer Sir Elton John, a close friend of David and Victoria, is the godfather of their sons, Brooklyn, Romeo, and Cruz.

THE JOURNEY CONTINUES

Beckham Mania was hitting full stride in the United States as David Beckham played his final game with Real Madrid in June 2007. Fans had waited since his official announcement in January, and now he was only weeks away from coming to the United States to begin his career with the Los Angeles Galaxy.

Television stations and cable shows were clamoring for interviews. Fans were snatching up tickets and Los Angeles Galaxy jerseys with Beckham's name on the back. There was also a constant update about Beckham's sore left ankle. Would it be healed enough for him to play when the Galaxy faced English power Chelsea in an exhibition game?

MAKING HIS AMERICAN DEBUT

The Galaxy's July 27 friendly game against Chelsea was televised nationally on ESPN, and the sports channel dedicated a camera to follow Beckham's every move. Fans watched every detail of the midfielder's performance, even the seventy-seven minutes he spent sitting on the bench watching his new teammates play.

The prestigious opponents hardly mattered to those in the stadium. All they wanted to see was Beckham take the field. Finally, in the seventy-eighth minute, Beckham ran onto the field to the delight of the capacity 27,000 fans in attendance. "The atmosphere is incredible," he said. "It made me feel a little embarrassed at times."[1]

DID YOU KNOW?

Beckham scored his first goal in MLS play on April 3 against the San Jose Earthquakes in the eighth minute. Beckham controlled a pass from Landon Donovan outside the penalty area and poked the ball past goalie Joe Cannon. In the thirty-seventh minute, Beckham set up a Donovan goal.

ESPN cameras followed Beckham's every move when he made his Galaxy debut.

WELCOME TO L.A.

In his very first start for the Galaxy, an August 15 SuperLiga match against D.C. United, Beckham scored his first goal in a Los Angeles uniform on a free kick in the twenty-seventh minute. Wearing the captain's armband, he also added an assist as the Galaxy won 2–0.

Each time Beckham touched the ball, cheers cascaded down from the stands. It was apparent that the ankle was still bothering him, though. He was unable to do much with the few touches he had and he did not attempt any risky tackles during his twelve minutes of action. But the fans did not care. They had come to see Beckham play.

Beckham's injury was not a concern for the Galaxy. The game was only an exhibition. However, the Galaxy had several important games coming up. Beckham was unable to play against FC Dallas in SuperLiga play, a tournament between MLS and Mexican first division teams. The ankle injury later worried England fans who wanted Beckham to play for England in a friendly against Germany in London's Wembley Stadium. Before Beckham could play for England, Galaxy coach Frank Yallop wanted him to play in a meaningful game for his team.

IF IT ISN'T ONE THING, IT'S ANOTHER

Los Angeles had known about the injured ankle before Beckham joined the team. Beckham had needed three injections in the ankle in order to play for Real Madrid in its season finale. However, the injury took longer to heal than expected.

Beckham's ankle eventually felt good enough for him to take the field. But his first season with the Galaxy would come to an unfortunate early end. Facing Mexican power Pachuca in the SuperLiga finals, Beckham was forced from the game in the thirtieth minute when he and Pachuca midfielder Fernando Salazar collided. Both players suffered knee injuries.

Beckham suffered a strained ligament and was told he would be out four to six weeks. That meant that Beckham, who had been able to play in only four of the team's twelve games since he'd joined in July, finished his first season with the Galaxy by playing a total of only five games.

INSTANT POPULARITY

It didn't take long for Beckham to become popular with American teenagers. He was named the top sports idol at the popular Teen Choice Awards, ahead of American stars such as Tiger Woods or Kobe Bryant.

REACHING A MILESTONE

As the calendar flipped from 2007 to 2008, Beckham could only hope his luck would change as well. The injuries to his ankle and knee ruined the end of his 2007 season and his debut with the Galaxy. By March, he was finally fully healthy.

He got some good news when he was called up to England's national team to play in a friendly against France. The game against France held special meaning for Beckham. When he took the field for England, he was making his 100th appearance for the national team.

Beckham became the fifth player to play at least 100 games for England, joining Billy Wright, Sir Bobby Charlton, Bobby Moore, and Peter Shilton. Despite losing the game 1–0, Beckham admitted that the contest was a special moment for him. "I was very emotional even during the build-up to the game today," he said. "I kept getting messages from family and friends about it and I had to hold back the tears. It was an emotional moment for myself and my whole family. They have been there for me through the ups and the downs and there have been more highs and lows."[2]

Once he became a fixture on the national team, one of Beckham's goals was to earn 100 caps for England. That goal had been accomplished. But, as of 2009, he still has some more goals he wants to achieve. A veteran of the 1998, 2002, and 2006

World Cups, Beckham wants to play in the 2010 World Cup to be held in South Africa and possibly break Shilton's record of 125 appearances for England.

"It is something I want to reach," said Beckham, who will be thirty-five when the 2010 World Cup finals start. "I would love to play and be part of the squad in 2010. But I'm taking it as it comes—who knows what is round the corner? The combination of the players and the combination of manager and staff is setting us up right for the qualification games for the World Cup."[3]

> ❝I would love to play and be part of the squad in 2010. But I'm taking it as it comes—who knows what is round the corner?❞
>
> —David Beckham

IS THE BECKHAM REVOLUTION WORKING?

In May 2008, Beckham had his best game in a Galaxy uniform. Facing the Colorado Rapids, he scored 2 goals on signature long, curving kicks to rally Los Angeles to a 2–2 tie. Both of his goals were classics.

The first came from twenty-five yards out. After receiving a pass, he controlled the ball and then launched it around a defender and by goalie Nick Rimando. The second goal came after Los Angeles

WHO SAYS SOCCER ISN'T POPULAR?

People still debate just how much of an effect Beckham has had on soccer in America. Judging by the attendance for Los Angeles games, he is having a tremendous effect. The average attendance for Galaxy games in 2008 was 28,000, more than English Premier League teams Reading, Portsmouth, Fulham, Blackburn, Wigan, and Bolton.

was awarded a free kick. Lining up twenty-nine yards from the goal, Beckham struck the ball and bent it around the wall of defenders and past a diving Rimando.

Beckham continued to play well for the Galaxy, but just how successful his move to the United States was began to be debated. With Beckham in the league, MLS experienced a surge in recognition in 2007. But was that surge still there in 2008? Had Beckham changed soccer forever in America? And did the world-famous star ever regret coming to the United States, where his fame was not on the same level it was in Europe and the rest of the world?

"I'm always going to miss playing in Europe," he said. "I did it for fifteen years at the highest level for two of the biggest clubs in the world, and I wanted to move to America and try and make an impact and have a new challenge. So I'm enjoying the challenge."[4]

Thanks in large part to Beckham, MLS was still experiencing a surge in 2008. Television ratings were up as was attendance and jersey sales. But the buzz that surrounded any Beckham event in 2007 was mostly gone in 2008. Fans still wanted to see him play, but the hype was no longer the same.

One reason for that may be that Los Angeles was struggling on the field. The club failed to make the playoffs in 2006 and 2007 and had a losing record since the arrival of Beckham. Los Angeles likes its stars, but it likes a winner more.

"We're past the honeymoon phase," said Tom Payne, the Galaxy's assistant general manager who oversees the business operation. "David's been a huge help, but it's not just open up the gates. We have to work hard."[5]

Because of the huge amount of hype surrounding Beckham's arrival to MLS, it was almost impossible for him or the league to live up to expectations. Beckham said he believed he made a difference in the league. However, he also said real change was not going to happen in one year.

"I think we've moved the needle slightly," he said. "I said when I first moved here that it's not going to take a year or two. It will take five or maybe ten years to make this league grow to a much higher level. You see many families turn up with their young

> **In ten years those kids are going to be fifteen and sixteen years old, turning around and saying 'I remember when we saw the Galaxy play.'**
>
> —*David Beckham*

kids and watch the Galaxy playing. In ten years those kids are going to be fifteen and sixteen years old, turning around and saying 'I remember when we saw the Galaxy play.' It might take that long, but hopefully we've made the footprint that obviously takes it further on."[6]

ON-FIELD STRUGGLES

Back on the field, the Galaxy continued to struggle in 2008 despite solid play by Beckham and Donovan. By August, Los Angeles hit a stretch in which it failed to earn a win in seven matches, leaving the team outside of a playoff berth. The Galaxy had a league-worst 7–12–8 record with three games remaining. For the third straight year, the team missed the playoffs.

BACK TO EUROPE

One of the drawbacks for Beckham playing for the Galaxy is the timing of the MLS season. It is nearly opposite of the European schedule, as games start in

BECKHAM IN 2008

GAMES	GOALS	ASSISTS
25	5	10

April and end in October. Most European leagues run from August through May or early June. International play then takes place mostly in the summer.

Beckham has made it clear he wants to continue playing for England, but in order to do so, England's manager, Fabio Capello, has said Beckham needs to stay in game shape. That is hard to do when not playing from November through March.

In order to stay in game shape during the off-season, MLS players often train with clubs in Europe. Beckham trained in Europe after the 2007 MLS season, but the experience served only as practice. He did not play in any meaningful games. So in October 2008, Beckham worked out a deal in which the Galaxy would loan him to AC Milan.

He would join the team for a few months and then return to Los Angeles before the start of the MLS season. While the loan would only be for a few months, some people speculated that the move was the first step for Beckham to get out of his contract with the Galaxy and return to Europe to finish out his career. One person who was not surprised about the temporary move was Beckham's former manager at Manchester United—Sir Alex Ferguson.

"It is hardly a surprise," Ferguson said. "Going to the United States does not get you the kind of football he is used to. It is not the right level of football, therefore coming back into the mainstream of the game is not a surprise."[7]

Several of the Milan players were looking forward to Beckham's arrival. Andriy Shevchenko praised Beckham as a great professional who still played the game at a high level. Filippo Inzaghi said Beckham would be welcomed to the team and be a benefit to the club.

But one person who questioned Beckham's move was Bruce Arena, the coach for the Galaxy. "On the surface, it sounds like an odd proposition," Arena said. "I don't see where that benefits MLS or the Galaxy. I would think that [given] the position the Galaxy is in and [the fact that] we're rebuilding our team and trying to have a successful year, it would seem very odd if we were loaning out our top players at the start of the season."[8]

HELLO MILAN

Beckham was officially introduced as an AC Milan player to the media in December, only days before Christmas. The event was once again big news. No matter where Beckham plays—Manchester, Madrid, Los Angeles, or Milan, he is big news. His official introduction brought out 150 journalists.

Beckham is introduced to the AC Milan crowd after it was announced he would be joining the team.

When AC Milan returned to the field in January 2009, Beckham quickly found success. To the surprise of many, Beckham cracked the starting lineup in his first Serie A match with Milan, against Rome on January 11. He went on to score 2 goals and get 2 assists in his first five games. Beckham continued to make an impact with Rossoneri, and soon made it clear that he would like to stay in Milan and not go back to the Galaxy.

After a long and highly publicized battle through the media, Beckham got his wish. Instead of returning to the Galaxy in March, Beckham would stay with Milan until the Italian season was over and join Los Angeles midway through the MLS season in July. MLS would also receive $10 million, with reportedly a good amount coming directly from Beckham. The star midfielder could terminate his contract after the 2009 MLS season. Beckham ended up playing in twenty games for AC Milan in the Serie A and UEFA Cup, scoring twice with 5 assists.

RETURNING TO AMERICA

David Beckham returned to the Galaxy for a July 16, 2009, game against the New York Bulls. Beckham was scoreless in the match, but the Galaxy won 3–1. A crowd of 23,238 showed up for the game at Giants Stadium in East Rutherford, New Jersey. That was higher than New York's average attendance, but about one-third the amount of fans who showed up for Beckham's debut in New York City two years before.

DID YOU KNOW?

In Beckham's fourth game back with the Galaxy, 93,137 fans came to the Rose Bowl in Pasadena, California, to watch the Galaxy play Spanish team Barcelona in a friendly. It was the biggest crowd to see a soccer game in the United States since the 1994 World Cup.

UNWELCOME RETURN

Some Galaxy fans were not necessarily happy to have Beckham back. These fans believed that Beckham turned his back on the Galaxy when he extended his loan at AC Milan. By extending his loan, Beckham was forced to miss part of the Galaxy's season.

In Beckham's first game back in Los Angeles—a friendly against his old team, AC Milan—a group of hardcore Galaxy fans called the Riot Squad booed the star player. Beckham confronted the group during halftime and was later fined for doing so.

After the game, Beckham downplayed the Riot Squad's reaction. "At the end of the day, I play my game," he said. "If it's not good enough for some people, as long as it's good enough for myself and the team, nothing else matters."

Even though the Riot Squad booed Beckham, most of the fans were supportive and happy to have him back.

Still, Beckham calls himself lucky. Others call him a world icon and others believe he is a gracious superstar ready to help those less fortunate. In the end, however, he is just David Beckham, a soccer player, father, and concerned citizen who has always strived to meet the next challenge, wherever it leads him in the world.

Whether or not Major League Soccer becomes one of the most popular professional sports leagues in the United States remains to be seen. However, Beckham's presence raised the league's profile worldwide and helped give the sport a real superstar to cheer for in the United States.

CAREER ACHIEVEMENTS

- Fourth Place—2001 European Footballer of the Year

- Second Place—2001 FIFA World Footballer of the Year

- 2001 BBC Sports Personality of the Year

- 2001 Britain's Sportsman of the Year

- 2001 Western Union Most Valuable Player

- 2000 Nationwide Football Awards Player of the Year

- Second Place—2000 World Footballer of the Year

- Second Place—1999 European Player of the Year

- 1997 PFA Young Player of the Year

- Helped lead Manchester United youth team to FA Youth Cup title in 1992

- Helped lead Manchester United to English Premier League titles in 1995–96, 1996–97, 1998–99, 1999–2000, 2000–01, 2002–03

- Helped lead Manchester United to FA Cup title in 1996 and 1999

- Helped lead Real Madrid to La Liga title in 2006–07

- Earned 100th cap for England in 2008 against France

- Led Los Angeles with 10 assists in 2008

- Named Major League Soccer Player of the Year in 2008 by ESPN

CAREER STATISTICS

Year	Team	Games*	Goals
1992–1993	Manchester United	4	0
1994–1995	Preston North End	5	2
	Manchester United	10	1
1995–1996	Manchester United	40	8
1996–1997	Manchester United	49	12
1997–1998	Manchester United	50	11
1998–1999	Manchester United	55	9
1999–2000	Manchester United	48	8
2000–01	Manchester United	46	9
2001–02	Manchester United	43	16
2002–03	Manchester United	52	11
2003–04	Real Madrid	43	6
2004–05	Real Madrid	38	4
2005–06	Real Madrid	41	5
2006–07	Real Madrid	31	4
2007	Los Angeles	5	0
2008	Los Angeles	25	5
2009	AC Milan	20	2

*Includes Domestic, Champions League, UEFA Cup, and League Cup appearances

FOR MORE INFORMATION

FURTHER READING

Beckham, David with Tom Watt. *Beckham: Boot Feet On The Ground*. New York: HarperCollins, 2003.

Harrison, Paul. *Star Files: David Beckham*. Chicago: Raintree, 2006.

Hunt, Chris. *The Complete Book of Soccer*. Buffalo, NY; Richmond Hill, Ont.: Firefly Books, 2006.

WEB LINKS

David Beckham's home page:
davidbeckham.com

Los Angeles Galaxy's home page:
lagalaxy.com

Major League Soccer's home page:
mlsnet.com

CHAPTER NOTES

CHAPTER 1. COMING TO AMERICA

1. Christine Brennan, "Beckham Looking Forward to U.S. Challenge," *ABC News*, January 12, 2007, <http://abcnews.go.com/GMA/sotry?id=2786923> (September 11, 2008).

2. Grant Wahl, "Vend It Like Beckham," *Sports Illustrated*, January 22, 2007, <http://vault.sportsillustrated.cnn.com/vault/article/magazine/MAG1106893/index.htm> (September 12, 2008).

3. "Coming to America," *Sports Illustrated*, January 11, 2007, <http://sportsillustrated.cnn.com/2007/soccer/01/11/beckham.mls/index.html> (September 11, 2008).

4. "MLS chief hails Beckham capture," *ESPNsoccernet*, January 11, 2007, <http://soccernet.espn.go.com/news/story?id=399497&cc=5901> (September 12, 2008).

5. Wahl, January 22, 2007.

6. "Beckham agrees to LA Galaxy move," *BBC Sports*, January 12, 2007, <http://news.bbc.co.uk/sport1/hi/football/6248835.stm> (September 13, 2008).

7. Jack Bell, "David Beckham Is Coming to America," *New York Times*, January 11, 2007, <http://www.nytimes.com/2007/-01/11/sports/soccer/12beckham.html> (September 12, 2008).

8. Grant Wahl," Kick Start," *Sports Illustrated*, August 15, 2005, <http://vault.sportsillustrated.cnn.com/vault.magazine/MAG1112308/index.htm> (September 12, 2008).

9. Kelly Whiteside, "Conquest of USA beckons to Beckham," *USA Today*, May 30, 2005, < http://www.usatoday.com/sports/soccer/world/2005-05-30-beckham-america_x.htm> (September 11, 2008).

CHAPTER 2. GROWING UP IN ENGLAND

1. Jeff Bradley, *World's Greatest Athletes: David Beckham*, Mankato, The Child's World, 2008, p. 9.

2. David Beckham, *Beckham: Both feet on the ground*, New York, CollinsHarper, 2003, p. 21

3. Ken Pendleton, *Sports Heroes and Legends: David Beckham*, Minneapolis, Twenty-First Century Books, 2007, p. 12.

4. Beckham, p. 35.

CHAPTER 3. STARTING HIS CAREER

1. David Beckham, *Beckham: Both feet on the ground*, New York, CollinsHarper, 2003, p. 55.

2. Ken Pendleton, *Sports Heroes and Legends: David Beckham*, Minneapolis, Twenty-First Century Books, 2007, p. 25

3. Jeff Bradley, *World's Greatest Athletes: David Beckham*, Mankato, The Child's World, 2008, p. 17.

4. "Manchester United boss Sir Alex Ferguson gives evidence in multi-million damages case," *The Mirror*, January 7, 2008, <http://mirror.co.uk/news/top-stories/2008/07/01/manchester-united-boss-sir-alex-ferguson-gives-evidence-in-multi-million-damages-case-89520-20627992/> (September 17, 2008).

5. Enda Brady, "Memories of David Beckham's Debut," *Sky News*, February 27, 2008, <http://news.sky.com/skynews/Home/Sky-News-Archive/Articles/20082851279137> (September 18, 2008).

6. Ibid.

7. Beckham, p. 69.

8. Ibid, p. 88.

CHAPTER NOTES

CHAPTER 4. A RISING STAR

1. Ken Pendleton, *Sports Heroes and Legends: David Beckham*, Minneapolis, Twenty-First Century Books, 2007, p. 38.

2. "Becks set to shoot on sight," *4TheGame.com*, February 10, 1997, <http://www.4thegame.com/club/manchester-united-fc/news/ 18703/BECKS+SET+TO+SHOOT+ON+SITE.html> (September 17, 2008).

3. David Beckham, *Beckham: Both feet on the ground*, New York, CollinsHarper, 2003, p. 121.

4. "Becks set to shoot on sight," February 10, 1997.

5. Ibid.

6. "Beckham feels the heat," *4TheGame.com*, September 16, 1997, <http://www.4thegame.com/club/manchester-united-fc/news/ 32787/BECKHAM+FEELS+THE+HEAT.html> (September 17, 2008).

7. Ibid.

8. "Wright pleads with Hoddle after qualification," *4TheGame.com*, October 12, 1997, <http://www.4thegame.com/club/manchester-united-fc/news/26081/WRIGHT+PLEADS+WITH+HODDLE+AFTER +QUALIFICATION.html> (September 17, 2008).

CHAPTER 5. FROM HERO TO GOAT

1. "Hoddle should have picked Beckham," *4TheGame.com*, June 22, 1999, <http://www.4thegame.com/club/manchester-united-fc/news/ 33586/HODDLE+SHOULD+HAVE+PICKED+BECKHAM.html> (September 17, 2008).

2. "Beckham's darkest hour," *UEFA.com*, n.d., <http://www.uefa.com/ magazine/news/kind=32/newsid=27844.html> (September 18, 2008).

3. "Beckham says sorry," *BBC News*, July 1, 1998, <http://news.bbc.co.uk/1/hi/sports/football/124372.stm> (Sept 17, 2008).

4. "Beckham's darkest hour," n.d.

5. Ibid.

6. Ibid.

7. Ibid.

8. David Beckham, *Beckham: Both feet on the ground*, New York, CollinsHarper, 2003, p. 143.

CHAPTER 6. REDEMPTION

1. David Beckham, *Beckham: Both feet on the ground*, New York, CollinsHarper, 2003, p. 215.

2. "Captain Becks ready to lead from the middle," *TheFA.com*, November 4, 2000, <http://www.thefa.com/England/SeniorTeam/NewsAndFeatures/Postings/2000/11/1042.htm> (September 20, 2008).

3. Beckham, p. 218.

4. Jeff Bradley, *World's Greatest Athletes: David Beckham*, Mankato, The Child's World, 2008, p. 26.

5. Ibid, p. 27.

6. "Eriksson hails captain Beckham," *BBC News*, October 6, 2001, <http://news.bbc.co.uk/sport1/hi/football/world_cup_2002/1580942.stm> (September 17, 2008).

7. "David Beckham's Line Of Enquiry," *BBC Radio*, December 12, 2007, <http://www.bbc.co.uk/pressoffice/pressreleases/stories/2007/12_december/24/beckham.shtml> (September 23, 2008).

CHAPTER NOTES

CHAPTER 7. OFF TO SPAIN

1. "Barcelona beckons," *SI.com*, June 10, 2003, <http://sportsillustrated.cnn.com/soccer/news/2003/06/10/beckham_tues/>(September 15, 2008).

2. "Beckham to join Real Madrid," *CNN.com*, June 17, 2003, <http://www.cnn.com/2003/WORLD/europe/06/17/beckham.madrid.deal/>(September 14, 2008).

3. Ibid.

4. "Real unveil Beckham," *BBC*, July 2, 2003, <http://news.bbc.co.uk/sport1/hi/football/3037824.stm> (September 15, 2008).

5. Ibid.

6. "Figo: 'Monster' Beckham," *The FA.com*, February 18, 2004, <http://www.thefa.com/England/SeniorTeam/NewsAndFeatures/Postings/2004/02/England_vPortugal_Feb04_FigoBecks.htm> (September 16, 2008).

7. Henry Winter and Sid Lowe, "With a flourish and a title, Beckham leaves Real Madrid," *The Age.com*, June 19, 2007, <http://www.theage.com.au/news/soccer/with-a-flourish-and-a-title-beckham-leaves-real-madrid/2007/06/18/1182019028673.html> (September 15, 2008).

CHAPTER 8. WORLD ICON

1. "Becks set to shoot on sight," *4thegame.com*, February 10, 1997, <http://www.4thegame.com/club/manchester-united-fc/news/18703/becks+set+to+set+on+sight.html>(September 16, 2008).

2. "Victoria helps me handle the spice of fame Beckham," *4thegame.com*, June 9, 1997, <http://www.4thegame.com/club/manchester-united-fc/news/19206/victoria+helps+me+handle+the+spice+of+fame+beckham.html> (September 16, 2008).

3. Stephen Moyes and Fiona Cummins, "Exclusive: My David By Ted Beckham," *The Mirror*, September 17, 2005, <http://www.mirror.co.uk/news/tm_objectid=16141726&method=full&siteid-94762&headline=exclusive–58–my-david-by-ted-beckham-name_page.html> (September 16, 2008)

4. Dan Wootton, "David Beckham dad says Victoria wants a daughter," *Newsoftheworld.com*, August 5, 2008, <http://www.newsoftheworld.co.uk/sport/article10464.ece> (September 17, 2008)

5. Moyes and Cummins, September 17, 2005.

6. Michael Y. Park, "David Beckham: I'm happiest on the field," *People.com*, August 4, 2008, <http://www.people.com/people/article/0,,20216489,00.html> (September 15, 2008)

7. Michelle Tauber, "Meet the Beckhams," *People.com*, June 9, 2003, <http://www.people.com/people/archive/0,20140261,00.html> (September 15, 2008)

8. Marian Salzman, "David Beckham," *Time Magazine*, April 26, 2004, <http://www.time.com/time/magazine/article/0,9171,994040,00.html> (September 17, 2008)

CHAPTER NOTES

CHAPTER 9. GIVING BACK

1. Tony Stevens, "Charity starts at home," *The FA.com*, March 10, 2006, <http://www.thefa.com/England/SeniorTeam/NewsAndFeatures/Postings/2006/03/England_Beckhamacademy.htm> (September 21, 2008)

2. "David Beckham joins Team UNICEF," *UNICEF.org*, January 12, 2005, <http://www.unicef.org/emerg/disasterinasia/index_24809.html> (September 21, 2008)

3. "David Beckham's Charity Work," *looktothestars.org*, N.D., <http://www.looktothestars.org/celebrity/49-david-beckham> (September 20, 2008)

4. Ibid.

5. Ibid.

6. Ibid.

7. Jessica Herndon, "David Beckham Bends it for Charity," People.com, November 5, 2007, <http://www.people.com/people/article/0,20158249,00.html> (September 15, 2008)

8. "David Beckham: Knife attack haunted my childhood," *The Scotsman*, August 19, 2008, <http://news.scotsman.com/latestnews/David-Beckham-Knife-attack-haunted.4402298.jp> (September 24, 2008)

CHAPTER 10. THE JOURNEY CONTINUES

1. Beth Harris, "Beckham's Galaxy debut short, spoiled by Chelsea," *USA Today*, July 7, 2007, <http://www.usatoday.com/sports/soccer/mls/2007-07-21-beckham-exhibition_N.htm> (September 13, 2008)

2. "Beckham makes it 100," *Beckhamzone.com*, March 27, 2008, <http://beckhamzone.blogspot.com/2008/03/beckham-makes-it-100.html> (September 15, 2008)

3. Ibid.

4. Billy Witz, "Beckham Is Playing Well, but Without the Buzz," *New York Times*, July 19, 2008, <http://www.nytimes.com/2008/07/19/sports/soccer/19beckham.html?pagewanted=print> (September 23, 2008)

5. Ibid.

6. "Former Manchester United hero David Beckham is doing it for the kids as his American Revolution really takes off," *The Daily Mail*, July 22, 2008, <http://222.dailymail.co.uk/sport/football/article-1037185/Former-Manchester-United-hero-David-Beckham-doing-kids-American-revolution-really-takes-off.html> (September 22, 2008)

7. "Sir Alex Ferguson not surprised by David Beckham's AC Milan move," *Times Online*, October 24, 2008, <http://www.timesonline.co.uk/tol/sport/football/premier_league/manchester_united/artcile5006125.ece> (December 27, 2008)

8. "Tom Dart and Nick Szczepanik, "LA Galaxy coach Arena enters debate over Beckham move," *Times Online*, October 24, 2008, <http://www.timesonline.co.uk/tol/sport/football/european_football/artcile5003769.ece> (December 27, 2008)

GLOSSARY

cap—An appearance by a player for his national team.

Champions League—A yearly tournament that brings together the top soccer clubs in Europe.

clean sheet—A term used when a goalie doesn't allow a goal during a game, recording a shutout.

corner kick—Kick that is awarded when the defending team plays the ball out of bounds behind its own goal line. The ball is kicked from the corner of the field closest to where the ball went out.

cross—Pass that goes laterally across the field.

end line (also called goal line)—The line running along the width of the field at each end.

extra time—Overtime session added to tie games in tournament play.

football—The British word for soccer.

free kick—Kick awarded by the referee for fouls outside the penalty area. Free kicks are taken at the spot of the foul. A free kick is also called a direct kick.

friendly—Another term for an exhibition game.

midfielder—A player who plays between the forwards and defenders.

penalty area—The area in front of the goal where the goalkeeper is allowed to use his or her hands. The area measures 18 yards by 44 yards.

penalty kick—Kick that is awarded to a player when an offensive player is fouled inside the penalty area.

Premiership—The top soccer league in England, also known as the English Premier League.

red card—A card shown to a player by a referee when he is ejecting the player from a game.

INDEX

INDEX